Scarborough

A Practical Guide for Visitors

by Jean Curd

Dalesman Books
1989

THE DALESMAN PUBLISHING COMPANY LTD.
CLAPHAM, via Lancaster, LA2 8EB

First published 1980

Third edition 1989

© Jean Curd 1980, 1989

ISBN: 0 85206 973 1

Maps by
J. J. Thomlinson

The publishers acknowledge the help
of Scarborough Tourism and Amenities
Department in preparing this new edition.

*In memory of Marjorie McLoughlin.
A visitor to Scarborough who enjoyed
watching busy children have fun.*

.

Printed in Great Britain by Peter Fretwell & Sons Ltd.
Goulbourne Street, Keighley, West Yorkshire BD21 1PZ.

Contents

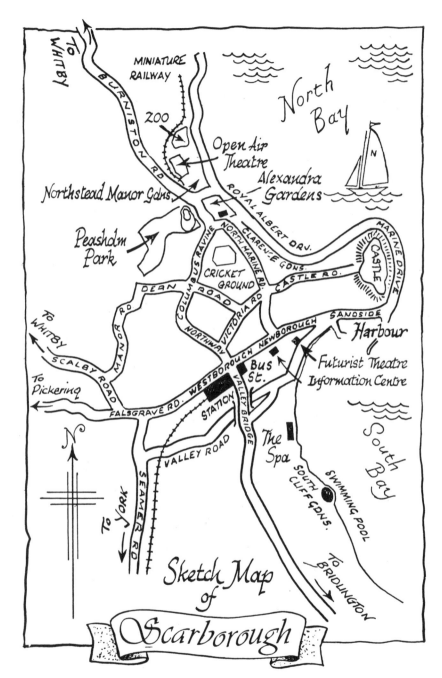

Sketch Map of **Scarborough**

(Kinderland, Mr Marvel's USA Fun Park and Water Splash World now occupy the Northstead Manor Gardens/Open Air Theatre area behind North Bay).

Visitors to the Town

VISITORS to Scarborough are usually people who have chosen to spend a holiday in this particular resort because it has so much to offer. The reasons for their choice are literally a hundredfold. Here they can find something to please everyone — it is just a matter of looking for it! This resort appeals to all ages including the very old as well as the very young; this gem of the Yorkshire coast provides many forms of energetic and soporific enjoyment. These include hill walks, hunting for history or simply lying or sitting in the warmth of the sun listening to music wafting on the breeze at the Spa. This part of the coast has for many years been a firm favourite for people from all walks of life whose homes are in the Midlands as well as Northern England.

In the past Scarborough has tempted the visitor from Scotland. This may have come about because at regular intervals the Scottish herring fleet used to move down the coast following the shoals of fish. On shore a great number of Scots girls followed the fleet and, at the landing ports, were occupied in cleaning, gutting and boxing the fish, whilst the fleet were offshore (this fact may have influenced many of their families to take a holiday in this area). In addition, Scarborough receives many visitors from the continent via Hull. Other regular visitors to Scarborough include those who use the fine facilities of the Spa as a conference centre. Scarborough Cricket Club, at the end of August, holds a cricket festival, while motor cycle racing (at national and international level) takes place at Oliver's Mount circuit.

Scarborough is poised to receive the visitor with a truly warm Yorkshire welcome. The facilities for making this visit a holiday to remember are here for the taking, and because of the vast number of diverse attractions the area is well supplied with leaflets obtainable at the town's Tourist Information Centre sited on St. Nicholas Cliff.

Two Views

A CLOSER look at Scarborough reveals many scenic views, the best of which can be seen as a panorama from the highest points at Oliver's Mount and the castle.

Oliver's Mount was so named because it was mistakenly thought that Oliver Cromwell placed his batteries on it during his seige of the castle in 1645. The mount is 500 feet above sea level and is crowned by a 75 feet War Memorial. From here to the west side of the town one can obtain a breathtaking view of part of the North York Moors National Park in the distance. Closer to the foot of the hill can be seen the Mere, a long stretch of water complete with pirate ship and other aquatic amusements, and certainly a very pleasant spot to enjoy a picnic or just have a change from sitting on the beach. As Oliver's Mount is so close to the resort the visitor can spend some time overlooking the world at work and play on land and on the sea. St. Mary's church and the castle ramparts make a fine backdrop to this scene.

In getting to Oliver's Mount by road the route, starting at the Railway Station, is to take the A165 Cayton and Filey road, cross the impressive Valley Bridge (approximately 70 feet above Valley Park), continue up Ramshill Road, past the traffic lights and turn to the right at Mountside.

The castle ramparts also reveal yet another side of Scarborough. This resort is fortunate enough to enjoy two magnificent bays, for the headland, on which the remains of the 12th century castle stand, divides the urban scene. It is from the castle that one can see the dividing line of land and sea, the splendours of towering cliffs, shrieking gulls on soaring wings and

The pirate ship on the Mere.

6

Scarborough Harbour and Castle from the pier (*photo:* Clifford Robinson).

crashing waves, majestic and all powerful. Below the ramparts to the south can be seen the full extent of this medieval town, stretching far below along the seashore to the Spa. To the north is the seemingly newer part of the town. The greatest urban growth took place here between 1851 and 1921 and the most rapid growth in the present century was during the inter-war period. However, much of this is hidden behind the cliffs and hotels of Queens Parade and North Marine Road, and it is only from the high vantage point of the castle grounds that the full expanse of the town can be seen. The extent of these views and those at Oliver's Mount are very much governed by the weather. Many of the visitors to the headland seem content with discovering the history of the castle that bears mute testimony to the stormy past, instead of looking towards the horizon where it is possible to see as far as Hayburn Wyke to the north and Cayton Bay to the south.

To gain access to the castle means a long steep walk from either bay, although it is possible to travel to the top of Castle Road by car and park along the side of St. Mary's church wall leaving only a short climb. It is worth noting that there is only limited parking in this vicinity and at busier times larger parking facilities can be found lower down Castle Road at the Queen Street or Castle road parking areas. However, parking here will still result in a long, but not so steep, walk to the castle.

From Early Times

IT MAY be easier to imagine that England was invaded by seafaring Norsemen, who would naturally land north of the Humber. Both written and archaelogical evidence leaves us with many avenues for discovering Scarborough's origins. One of the most important facts about this part of Yorkshire is that before the invading forces settled here, early Iron Age settlers found that the promontory provided an easily defended site. Within the castle walls there is also evidence of a Roman signal station (A.D. 367-394).

At the end of this era there came invaders from several directions, the greater proportion of whom appear to have been Anglian and Scandinavian. These have left us with many indicative place names — dale, gill, beck, thorpe. The founding of the present town now called Scarborough took place in A.D. 967. It was earlier thought that it meant 'the stronghold on the rocky face' or the 'stronghold of the skaroi.' The former was derived from the Old English sceard meaning cleft. The latter is from the Old Norse meaning an open edge or cleft; also skaroi is thought to be an old Nordic name meaning a man with a hair lip. This settlement was destroyed by the Normans and was not rebuilt until the second quarter of the 12th century, and so is not mentioned in the Domesday Book.

The castle and church were known to have been established by the Normans, for in 1189 the Abbot of Citeaux was granted, under the command of Richard Coeur de Lion, the revenues of this church. The church was to remain in the control of the Cistercian order for 200 years. The castle of course held the seat of power in the area, but it is documented that many of the lands around the promontory were still held by people with Scandinavian names. The town surrounded by walls began to thrive. By 1163 Scarborough had been granted a charter, and markets were held on the sands of the foreshore. The settlement soon spread and expanded beyond the walls into Newborough. A harbour area was in use, the first quay being built in 1252, but long before this fishing and smuggling were known to have taken place. Vincent Pier was rebuilt in 1732 and work on building the East Pier started in 1752. The West Pier — previously two island piers built of wood and stone — was replaced by the present structure in 1822.

During this time innovation was aiding the growth of the town, although the difficult land approach limited its character and development until 1626. A chance discovery by a Mrs. Farrow added a new facet to the town. A medicinal spring coming out of the foot of the cliffs (now the South Bay) was found to have great beneficial qualities. A certain Dr. Robert Wilkie in 1667

The Spa Bridge, as it looked when newly built in 1827.

claimed that the waters were a cure for at least thirty diseases as well as 'a most sovereign remedy against Hypochondiach Melancholly and windiness.' Scarborough Spaw (Spa) was an attraction indeed, for the area was not then known as a coastal resort. This came at the end of the 17th century when both adverse publicity and the curative qualities of the water were questioned, and the pressure of those who wanted to take the waters forced the hand of the local corporation into some organisation of the facilities.

In 1698 a cistern was built to collect the water and within two years a Spa-house was constructed. A cripple called Dicky Dickinson was appointed 'Governor of the Spaw.' He was directed to collect subscriptions of seven shillings and sixpence a season, and keep law and order. The spring's source was lost for two months when an acre of the cliff top slipped down the cliff face in 1737. This did not halt the progress of the small coastal town. A new pump house was built and lasted until 1851 when a splendid pavilion and formal gardens were commissioned to be built by Sir Joseph Paxton (of Crystal Palace fame). The gardens still survive although the original Spa buildings were destroyed by fire and rebuilt by Thomas Verity in 1876. Bathing machines had also been introduced by 1735. The attractions of Spaw water and sea bathing were now to make this coastal town one of the earliest of the new resorts by the sea.

Soon visitors were flocking to the Spa and the fine sandy beaches. The town, so long a collection of medieval streets, slowly expanded with the popularity of this new resort. The road from the town to the Spa was tortuous until in 1826 the Cliff Bridge Company was formed and the Spa Bridge was built. This, together with the incline lift, the first of three in the South Bay, offered the visitor a more congenial way to the Spa. The railways too were replacing the turnpike road systems, and in 1845 Scarborough had its first direct link with York. Many of the visitors to the Spa were from all over Northern England and beyond. It had been noted that Lady Sarah, Duchess of Marlborough, as well as exalted members of the peerage, the nobility and gentry were attracted here during the middle of the 18th century. The hotels and inns on the south part of the town were of impressive quality, and the more expensive were now being built round St. Nicholas Cliff and Newborough. The Grand Hotel was opened in 1867 and Scarborough was established as 'The Queen of Watering Places.'

The Grand Hotel, opened in 1867.

Arriving and getting around

WHILST at home the major decision of where to stay may have already been made, but if not the Tourist Information Centre at St. Nicholas Cliff will help. The next step will be to plan routes to and around the resort. For the rail traveller, and there are still many of them, the railway is in the heart of the town with its many shops. On stepping out of the station it would be easy to imagine that one was in a provincial town, but confirmation that you have at last arrived is provided by the bracing sea breezes. For those who need further public transport, local buses run from Central Bus Station which is only a few yards away on the corner of Somerset Terrace and Valley Bridge Road.

Visitors who travel to Scarborough by coach and car cross a hinterland full of incredibly beautiful views. So often passengers will only look through the windscreen, but because many of these roads hold hidden scenes of beauty and majesty it is well worth looking round during the journey. It would, for instance, be a pity to discover the beauty of the North York Moors at the end of the visit. The main routes into the town are the A165 coastal road from Hull and the A64 from York, while the A174 and A171 provide access from Teesside. There are alternative routes, but before taking them the traveller would be well advised to consider the capabilities of the car or coach as well as the classification of the road.

If the holiday-maker is flying into the area the nearest airports are the Leeds/Bradford Airport or the Teesside Airport, and then on by road or rail. North Sea ferries link the continent to this coastline sailing from Rotterdam or Zeebrugge and arriving at Hull.

Scarborough is in easy daily reach of many of the towns and cities in the Midlands and Northern England and so attracts many visitors for a day. If you have travelled by coach it must be remembered that there are three main coach parks — Valley Road, south of the town centre on the A64; William Street, which is the most central and nearest to the Scarborough cricket ground; and Burniston Road, north of the town centre on the A165. William Street and Burniston Road coach parks are close to the sea, being less than quarter of a mile from the North Bay.

Many holiday-makers who bring their own car find that walking is by far the quickest way to get to the most interesting places in the town. Scarborough has twelve listed car parks scattered over the central part of the town. For those who wish to spend the day on or near the North Bay there are many parking places along Marine Drive (room for 450 cars) and Royal Albert Drive (room for 450 cars). For those who prefer the South Bay area, parking for 176 cars is available in an underground car park at the end of

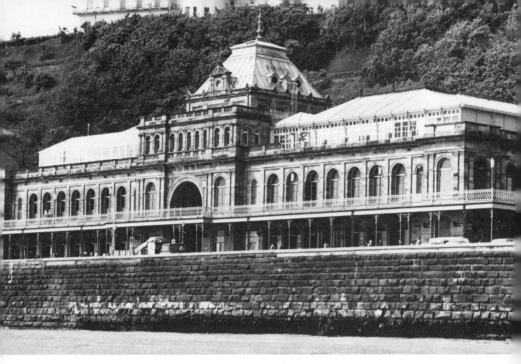

The imposing facade of Scarborough Spa (*photo:* Dennis Dobson).

Valley Road near the entrance to the Spa. The Spa itself has space for 170 cars, whilst the West Pier has space for 90. Most of the car parks are Pay & Display — notices are displayed at all car parks as appropriate. There is a short stay car park in North Street. For free parking the best areas are in the streets around Queens Parade in the north, centrally around Westborough, and in the streets behind the Esplanade on the South Cliffs. These parking areas are in narrow streets surrounded by guest houses and hotels so it is advisable to park with care and consideration.

A one-way traffic system is now operating in part of the town centre and motorists should look out for signs and directions — a leaflet is available at the Information Centre. The vast number of pedestrians and the steep inclines of some of the streets can lead to frustration, so therefore please drive carefully so that you and others may enjoy the holiday. To get from the South to the North Bay, the easiest and most exciting route is by the Marine Drive. Here the sea-covered rocks, rarely fully exposed, cause waves to break and sea spray to cascade in the air, often catching the motorist or pedestrian unawares. For the pedestrian, movement round the central part of the old town is through narrow streets with many occasions for looking down narrow alleys and flights of steep steps. In the past these would have supplied the local inhabitants, mostly fishermen, with speedy access to the beach and harbour, and today are well worth using.

Onto the Beaches

SCARBOROUGH, as mentioned before, has many attractions, not least of all its beaches, some of which are to be enjoyed and others treated with caution. These stretch from Scalby Mills in the north for almost four miles south past the Spa to Wheatcroft Cliff in the South Bay. The beaches have separate identities reflected in the amenities available and the popularity of the various attractions.

The North Bay

A chair lift links Scalby Mills with Northstead Manor Gardens and a miniature railway also connects the two, both operating regularly throughout the season. Under the cliffs a row of beach-huts line the promenade. The sands here are not always covered by the tide and it is often possible at high water to walk along the water's edge from Scalby Mills to the Corner Cafe. Behind the cliffs is Kinderland — a large children's activity centre — and Mr. Marvel's USA Fun Park — a theme park for children of all ages! Here too, just a few hundred yards from the beach, is a heated outdoor swimming pool and water theme park and just up a hill a new indoor pool. Near the beaches of the North Bay a red warning flag sometimes indicates that offshore swimming is dangerous, although the sands are ideal for the usual beach sports such as football, cricket or sandcastle making. In parts, the sands have outcrops of rocks and pools where children can spend happy hours fishing. A word of caution here — the closer you are to the headland, the less time you have available for beach activity.

Amusements along the sea front in the North Bay are relatively sparse. In the 1890s attempts were made to make this side of the town more attractive, but these ventures failed due to lack of finance and the fierceness of the sea. A pier was erected in 1869 and by 1890 the Royal Albert Drive completed the picture of a truly Victorian resort. Unfortunately, the North Bay pier was destroyed by the sea in 1905 and was never replaced, although by this time Clarence Gardens with their criss-cross footpaths were well established and have survived to the present day. Financially the area was doomed because of the lack of communication with the South Bay. It was not until 1908, when Sandside in the harbour area had been redesigned, that things improved. A road was built through the tangle of old buildings in the old part of the town and round the promontory at the foot of the cliffs; this was to be the Marine Drive. To complete the road 14,050 concrete blocks were needed to build a sea wall of 1,100 yards to a maximum height of 40 feet. Some of the blocks weighed up to nine tons. In the space behind the wall a quarter of a million tons of filling was needed to construct the 60 foot combined footpath and carriageway.

Between the two beaches is the harbour complex which is mentioned later in the text.

The South Bay

Adjoining the harbour is the popular centre of Scarborough, the amenities having long been established on the south side of the headland. It is here that the castle, high on the skyline, and the town below merge into the charm and antiquity of this part of England. In sharp contrast, the sea-shore has nearly a mile of shops, arcades, amusements and the new Olympia Ice Rink. Quay Street, once the home of shipbuilding, now stands away from but parallel to the sea-shore, the ship-yards having originally extended along the foreshore. This is now the area from the East Pier to Castlegate. The site was littered with ship timber and there was no road as such for the sands swept up to the buildings. The craft, many of barque class as well as the Yorkshire coble, were built on cradles and launched from incline planes on completion. One of the last to be launched was the *Clyde* in 1863 from the William Tyndall Yard. Evidence of the family can be found in St. Mary's churchyard which stands below the castle walls. Other shipbuilding families were Hewerd and Wharton, John Skelton, William Newham, George Dalesmith and G. W. Porritt. A lasting memory of the latter — Porritts Lane

Shipbuilding, once a feature of Quay Street and the South Bay.

14

— runs close to a famous inn, The Three Mariners. This house, now a museum, dates from 1300 and has a fine example of a 17th century gable and a 15th century door.

Moving along Sandside, the foreshore overlooks the fine dry sand that is seldom covered by the sea. It is here that a small area of beach has suitable entertainment for the smaller child. Also, hereabouts can be found stalls selling really fresh fish. The South Bay has always provided safe bathing, and it was near the end of St. Nicholas Cliff that the first bathing machines were kept as early as 1700. Opposite the beach long verandas still hold seating for those who prefer merely to watch. Nearing the Spa, the Valley

Scarborough Castle from the Harbour.

15

Road, crossed by its impressive footbridge, connects the town to the shore. Here the gardens set out on the banks of the main ravine contain many varieties of lawn and ornamental plantings.

The beach below the Spa is filled with sheltered spots surrounded by rocks and pools. It is beneath the Spa that many of the 'regular' holiday-makers find peace and relaxation within the shelter of the cliffs and buildings. To the south of the Spa is the South Bay open air bathing pool, standing on the slight plateau above the beach. Landward from this point the South Cliff gardens beckon. Here, perched on the top of the cliff, the Holbeck and Italian Gardens (fine examples of Sir Joseph Paxton's work) can be seen; they still have an air of peace and tranquillity.

Regular visitors to the resort usually have a favourite beach spot, some emphatically insisting on using one bay and not the other. It would be advisable, however, to consider more than the beach and its amenities. The direction of the prevailing wind is of major consideration. The North Bay

South Bay, on one of those "shimmering" days of summer *(photo: Clifford Robinson).*

beaches can be very windy, although westerly winds prevail in winter, summer and autumn, and often the South Bay near the Spa is a little more sheltered. Sometimes the visitor to Scarborough is dismayed to find that the coast line is shrouded in mist, locally called a 'sea fret.' When this happens it is a good idea to go inland for your amusement.

The Harbour

THE PORT has, from earliest written evidence, been of interest to people in high places. In 1225 a grant of 40 oaks was made by Henry III to the men of Scarborough for use in the harbour. By charter in 1251 a new harbour was to be built in timber and stone, and authority was given to its fishermen to land fish in Normandy without paying the toll. Elizabeth I granted 100 tons of timber and six tons of iron together with the sum of £500 towards rebuilding. By 1732 some 300 ships were using the harbour and George II passed an Act to enlarge it. The new section, named after its engineer William Vincent, now stands as his memorial. At this time coal was landed here from Newcastle and by 1752 plans for the East Pier had been made by Mr. Vincent. It was built by the consulting engineer John Smeaton, famous for his Eddystone lighthouse, who also had plans to prevent silting in the harbour. He proposed to cut a channel called a ducker hole through the shore at the end of the Old Pier, its object being to allow the silt to be washed out of the harbour by the tide. The ducker hole was made but some years later was filled in. The silt was then cleared manually, and later by bucket dredgers. In 1952 the council had a permanent dredger built to maintain a harbour deep enough to allow vessels of up to 1,000 tons.

In 1822 two previous island piers were replaced by the West Pier. By 1901, as previously mentioned, Sandside and the Marine Drive had been constructed to connect North and South Bays. The edge of the harbour was naturally Quay Street, evidence of this in the form of mooring posts having been found in the cellars of the houses.

The dangers of the sea and coastline together with the difficulties of entering the harbour resulted in the construction of a lighthouse. The first reference detailed that a signal flag was displayed by night and day when the water was above 12 feet deep. Later additions took place in 1840 when a cupola and second storey were built. The lighthouse suffered German bombardment in 1914 and was eventually rebuilt in 1931. A plaque commemorating its reconstruction can be seen on the present structure.

During the years of the harbour's growth, exports have included corn, butter, hams and salt fish. Imports have been brandy, wines, hemp, flax, coal, timber and iron (1796). In the decade prior to this, 1,500 seamen belonged to the port and the East India Service provided jobs for 500. The harbour participated in the rapid growth of the herring industry, but a

Opposite: **Waiting for the tide in Scarborough's harbour (photo: Clifford Robinson).**

decline in the number of shoals since 1970 has resulted in a complete ban on landing this fish. The present fishing industry is divided into two seasons: in the winter season, October to March, catches are of white fish only, whereas the summer season sees the white fish supplemented by shell fish.

Whilst looking at the fishing vessels in the harbour it will be noticed that there are two different types, keel boats and coble craft. Keel boats usually fish by trawler method whilst cobles fish from lines up to 600 feet long, supported by buoys and baited at intervals. Both types of vessels fish mainly on a daily basis in winter, but during the summer may well stay at sea for three or four days. Daily fish auctions are held on West Pier, a hand bell being rung to attract the buyers when the fish is landed. When a catch is auctioned it is despatched to towns all over the country, the buyers transporting their own goods and providing their own boxes. Ice is available at the harbour market so that the fish can arrive at its destination in peak condition.

Other regular callers to the harbour are commercial vessels carrying cargoes such as timber, wheat, fertilisers and barley. Chemicals and hardboard too have been handled. Recent annual statistics show that 81 vessels handled 50,005 tons of timber, 18 tons of sheepskins, 141 tons of iron ore and 6,259 tons of potatoes. The sight of these cargo vessels is impressive and it is well worth watching the unloading. The East Harbour, contained within the East Pier and Old Pier, is a safe mooring for many light craft. Pleasure trips can be taken on the *Regal Lady,* which runs hourly trips (May to September). There are also speed boats, motor boats (for fishing trips) and rowing boats available from the harbour slipway.

Close to West Pier with its fish market and gutting sheds can be found the Lifeboat Station. During the summer months holiday-makers are welcome to walk round and look at the powerful boat. Scarborough's present lifeboat is the *Amelia,* a 37 foot self-righting Oakley type. The station crew practise a launch at least once every six weeks. If they are called out to face the dangers of a sea rescue, the inshore crew will take over the duties until assistance arrives from another station.

A Town Trail

AWAY from the beaches, Scarborough through its unique history displays many parks, buildings and streets of interest. These are not limited to specific areas of the town, although it is true to say that many of the older buildings are confined to streets in the shadow of the castle headland. Other areas of the town have examples of 19th and 20th century buildings. Those of most interest can be seen by following a town trail.

A suggested start for such a trail is at the Tower Cottage on Mulgrave Terrace (the castle end of Castle Road). In the wall on the left is a well weathered sandstone plaque which states:

      'Hinderwell Fountain

      Near this place stood a fountain . . .'

The cottage itself was built in 1865 and the group of houses in this part of the Castle Road were constructed in castellated Gothic style to 'fit in' with the ruined castle on the hill.

Walking towards St. Mary's Church, the graves of Anne Brontë (one of the famous Brontë sisters) and H. L. Tindal, 1851, of shipbuilding fame can be found in this part of the cemetery. St. Mary's church was once a little bit of France in England. It was owned by the Cistercian monks of Citeaux, who

St. Mary's Church.

21

had the right to extract a tenth (or tithe) of the fish and land in the parish.

Cross Church Lane into the main churchyard; it is well to note that St. Mary's has been the town's parish church for 800 years. During the summer months historical pre-recorded information is available whilst visiting the church. Visitors are made most welcome, with tea or coffee being served by the parishioners. Walking round to the south door there is an inscription in Latin which when translated reads: 'A large number of citizens, and as many strangers, collected money and in 1750 restored with amazing exertion and care, a building dedicated to Mary, which had been spoilt wrongfully a long time ago at the time of Cistercians.'

Within the church there are housed many plaques dedicated to mariners (most of them have been brought from St. Thomas's sited down the hill which has now closed but was once the sailor's church). The interior with its chapels dedicated to St. Nicholas, the patron saint of mariners, and St. Stephen, the first Christian martyr, is full of interest for visitors. **Leaving the**

Stained glass in one of the south windows of St Mary's Church (*photo:* A. Hall).

22

church by the south door, take the centre path and make your way down the steps leading to Church Stair Steps. On this flight once stood cottages; when there was no piped water supply or drains, waste water from the buildings was thrown into wide gutters at each side of the steps.

Just carry on walking and you come to a lane called Paradise. To the right is the Graham Sea Training School once famous all over the world. The house (built in late 18th and early 19th centuries) is reputed to be the birth place of Sir George Cayley, 'the father of British aviation.' If you want a pleasant half-day out, go to Brompton, a village nearby where Cayley flew the first ever 'aeroplane.' As you walk along Paradise, notice to the left the churchyard wall which is unusual. It is of 18th century brick capped with 19th century glazed tiles lying on footings of stone. Further along you can see the coastguard cottages which command a view across the harbour and the South Bay.

Now dropping quickly down the steep slope from Paradise into Castlegate (the term 'gate' from the old Scandinavian word meaning street) and on to Burr Bank, you will have crossed two well-known Scarborough streets — Longwestgate and Princess Street. To those more deeply interested there are many fine examples of historic architecture. In Longwestgate these include No. 68, a good early 18th century house with carved upper corners to the window openings; No. 72, Jason House, an 18th century fairly large house; and No. 123, once a vicarage built about 1820. Many of these buildings have suffered from demolition, rebuilding and infilling. Princess Street still holds the atmosphere of past times, examples of fine Georgian architecture including curved external steps to first floor entrances, boot scrapers and embossed iron coal hole lids.

It will be noticed that most of the main streets are parallel and follow the ridge from the castle. They are connected by narrow alleys or steps leading down to the harbour. At Burr Bank you can look over the roof tops and have a magnificent view over the harbour — roofscape can give a new perspective to old scenes. Pantiles have been the usual roofing material in this area, giving a rich red appearance to the scene.

Walk down East Sandgate turning left into Whitehead Hill and then into Quay Street. This was once an ancient and busy street and an artist's paradise. Now you will see it has changed considerably. The house on the corner, No. 2, is a good example of a timber-framed 16th century building.

Turn right into a small alley leading to the Bethel Mission, once a meeting place for sailors and fishermen. Carry on to the end of the alley and you will be in Sandside. As previously stated, it was once the site of Scarborough Fair and Market, now remembered in the well-known ballad, the origins of which probably stem from the early times of the Fair. Space was so scarce that activities such as these were situated almost on the beach. On Sandside is the 16th century stone-built gabled house believed to have been used by King Richard III. It has been much altered, having once held a small museum, and is now used as a cafe.

Now return along Sandside in the direction of a public house called the

Newcastle Packet, which probably has links with the import of coal landed in 1732. This inn was largely rebuilt in 1898, but in a narrow passage you can see some old beams which form part of the 13th century cruck framing. It was here sailors used to wait for their boats, or for a storm to abate. In the timbers they carved their initials just as people today write on walls.

Walk in East Sandgate towards St. Thomas's church. It was from here that many of the plaques dedicated to mariners were moved to St. Mary's church. Just before you reach the church door, look for a small alleyway called 'The Bolts.' This narrow passage runs along parallel to Foreshore Road. Really it is a sort of secret passage and if you are ever in a hurry go this way, as it avoids all crowds. Further along this passage you may notice how close the houses are. In past times doors opened into the passages and due to the lack of direct daylight the rooms would be very dark. The first break in this narrow alley brings you to Custom House Steps, a name taken from the house at the top.

A few paces away from the steps, turn right into the continuation of Bolts. On the right you may see gates marked 'boatyard.' This has long since gone, and a car park now occupies this site. Once herrings were smoked on this site and the building was known as the Kipper Houses.

Emerging from the Bolts you come into Eastborough, once called Merchants' Row. **With your back to the sea walk uphill and the road bears to**

Panorama from Church Stair Steps.

the left. Look out for a flight of steps on the left, which descend between houses and shops to Foreshore Road. **Take the second flight.** As you will see this too is a speedy direct route to the harbour area. These steps have probably been used as a safe place for children to play in, out of wind and weather, for many generations. About halfway down notice to the right and left another alley that runs at right angles to the steps, a similar alley to the Bolts. Until 1950 this was its continuation but owing to vandalism it was closed by the property owners. The Bolts was a direct and continuous route in early times from St. Thomas's church through to St. Thomas's Hopsital.

Continue down the steps to Foreshore Road, emerging opposite the Lifeboat Station. The crew are expected to have a practice launch once every six weeks. The station is open for visitors to look around the life saving appartus during the summer months; also on show are accounts of dramatic rescues.

Now turn to walk to West Pier and, approaching the Harbour Master's office, look at the harbour basin. The wharf that runs parallel to the road is called New Wharf; in early times ships were built on cradles and were launched on incline planes so it was necessary to have a wharf. As time went by a stone harbour was built with capstan rings driven into the walls for mooring. Here the harbour wall at the bottom of the slipway shows evidence of the changes that have taken place. To see this it is necessary to become a mudlark, and if you do the following rules must be obeyed:

1   Make sure the tide is out and not on the turn.
2   Keep close to the wall as this is the driest place.
3   Do not approach the hull of any boat in the area.

A few yards under New Wharf can be seen steps that are concreted up due to the expansion of the site needed for herring gutting. Stay close to the wall and you will see many examples of rings used for mooring boats, some of these still being complete with shackle.

If you have not taken the above route then walk towards the North Bay and just 50 yards ahead you will see another slipway.

As you emerge there is aother slipway. Cross Sandside — there you will find one of the few remaining boat builders of Scarborough. This boatyard still makes cobles as well as the small warships used in the famous model naval battle held at Peasholm Park.

Turn left from the boatyard, enter Porrits Lane and at the top of here you are back again in Quay Street. Some of the old retired fishermen will tell you that many years ago huge blocks of ice, so clear that you could see through them, were stored in this part of the street. These blocks were cut from ice in the fiords of Norway and were kept cold by being stowed in the hulls of boats. The ice when landed was covered with sacking until cut up and used for packing fish or selling to the ice-cream makers of the time.

Move along Quay Street towards the Three Mariners Inn, sited at the end of Dog and Duck Lane. This famous inn dates from 1300 and has a 17th century gable and 18th century doorway. During your progress along this street, there are many changes in building styles and the roadway becomes very enclosed and has more than a close resemblance to the Bolts. One could well surmise that this street may once have been its continuation as they follow the same line.

Now you step into Marine Drive at the Toll Bar; the North Bay is to your left, the South Bay, St. Nicholas Cliff and the Spa at your right. In the South Bay in the area of the Railway Station past St. Nicholas Cliff top to Newborough and southward to the Esplanade, overlooking the Spa, there are many fine architectural examples of Regency and Victorian Scarborough, including The Grand Hotel, the first of its kind. This is the most impressive of Scarborough's hotels and was built 1862-7. Close by a plaque marks the site of a house where Anne Brönte died in 1849.

The list of noteworthy buildings is endless. Most are covered in a survey of streets and buildings entitled *The Streets of Scarborough* by Raymond Fieldhouse and John Barrett, 1973, published by Scarborough and District Civic Society.

Trackers References
Berrymen, B., *Scarborough as it was.*
Edwards, M. (ed.), *Scarborough 966—1966.*
Fieldhouse, R. and Barrett, J., *The Streets of Scarborough.*
H.M.S.O., *Scarborough Castle.*
King, O. A. M., *The Scarborough District* (in the British Landscapes Through Maps Series: The Geographical Association).
Rowntree, A., *A History of Scarborough.*
Rutter, J. G., *Historic Scarborough.*
The Local Room of Scarborough Public Library and the Rotunda Museum, Vernon Road, should be visited.

Parks and Gardens for Entertainment

MANY of the resort's parks have already been mentioned in the text, but it is worth noting that there are about 600 acres of parks, gardens, and public open places, each having its own appeal.

Peasholm Park is one of the most popular attractions, and within it one can enjoy the peace and serenity of Peasholm Glen, whilst close by is another area for motor launches, row boats and canoes. Mini naval warfare, inspired by the historic Battle of the River Plate, is enacted twice weekly. Water skiing displays are given on Tuesday evenings (May-August). The central island of the lake is invitingly illuminated in the evenings and both daylight and dusk strolls can be taken in Tree Walk Wonderland.

Alexandra Gardens in the North Bay has a new Indoor Bowls Complex.

Northstead Manor Gardens embraces the Open Air Theatre, as well as Kinderland, Mr. Marvel's Showtime U.S.A. Fun Park, Water Splash World, boating lake and miniature railway.

The Mere is a water sports centre with picnic areas, Treasure Island and the Hispaniola pirate ship, rowing boats and canoes, putting green, cafe.

Holbeck and Italian Gardens in the South Bay have the peace and tranquility of secluded ornamental gardens.

Oliver's Mount is an outstanding viewpoint comparable with the best in Britain.

Falsgrave Park is situated between Seamer Road (A64), Falsgrave Road and Springhill Lane and contains about thirteen acres of parkland. From its highest point there are excellent views of Oliver's Mount and the Mere.

Lovers of **golf** have the choice of two clubs, North Cliff or South Cliff, and these clubs have an open golf week in September. Scarborough Sports Centre, Filey Road, has some fine facilities.

Anglers too enjoy an annual festival during September. Rock angling from piers, rocks or beaches is supplemented by boat angling. The boat's helmsman usually knows the best of the inshore fishing spots. For those visitors who find that the sea is not inviting enough for swimming, there is an indoor pool adjacent to the car park on the corner of Burniston Road and Northstead Manor Gardens (the entrance to the pool is off Ryndle Crescent). There are two outdoor pools, one in South Bay near the Spa, and the other situated in the North Bay close to the beach and Northstead Manor Gardens.

Opposite: **Scarborough's South Bay by night** (*photo:* **John Edenbrow**).

Scarborough is well blessed with entertainment centres for the twilight hours. It can boast a wide range of theatres, the most famous of which — 'Theatre in the Round' — owes its popularity to the resident playwright Alan Ayckbourn. Many of his plays have had their world premiere here before moving to the West End of London. Night life in Scarborough abounds with a wide range of pubs and night clubs, cinemas and 'penny arcades'.

Clock Tower in Holbeck Gardens.

Places to visit by car

SCARBOROUGH is fortunate in being situated between Whitby and Bridlington, and so the visitor has a choice of direction when wanting to explore other interesting parts of the coastline or hinterland. The best way of visiting some of these places is by car.

North from Scarborough

Leaving the town on the A171, **Scalby** and **Hackness** are the first two places that offer variety and interest. Hills rise steeply behind Scalby, once the site of an army camp (World War I, with fire shooting butts), and form **Silpho Moors**. Here there are many well signposted forest walks. **Hackness** has a Saxon cross and a beautifully preserved 13th century church with many medieval furnishings. Northward on the coast road lie **Cloughton** and **Burniston**, both villages having footpaths that lead to excellent facilities for fishing and bathing.

The A171 crosses the eastern side of the North York Moors to the adjacent villages of **Fylingthorpe** and **Robin Hood's Bay.** The coastline here has suffered extensive damage by erosion, threatening to tip the ancient port of Robin Hood's Bay into the sea (for further information on the village see the Dalesman Mini Book). From here the coast road leads to **Whitby** (well worth a visit), whilst B1416 will lead to **Ruswarp.** This is the first village that lies outside of Whitby on the River Esk.

Within a radius of six miles of Whitby there are many villages of interest, the most northerly being **Runswick Bay** and **Staithes** on the A174. They are the haunts of artists, for these fishing villages have many original houses that cling to the side of steep cliffs. The beach at Runswick is easily accessible with parking facilities close by. **Hinderwell** derives its name from St. Hilda's Well, which is still visible in the churchyard. Just outside the village the second highest cliff in England can be seen, Boulby Cliff.

Inland from Whitby lie Arncliffe woods on the south side of the Esk valley. At **Glaisdale,** on the western edge of the woods, can be found an early 17th century packhorse bridge known as Beggar's Bridge. The moors around here reach up to 1,400 feet above sea level. Much of **Goathland** village is of this century, but it is well recorded in history for it is close to **Wheeldale** with its Roman road. Nearby are **Beckhole, Nelly Ayre Foss** and **Darnholme,** places of beauty that help to make this one of the finest parts of the National Park.

West from Scarborough

Travelling inland on A170, the first villages are **East** and **West Ayton.**

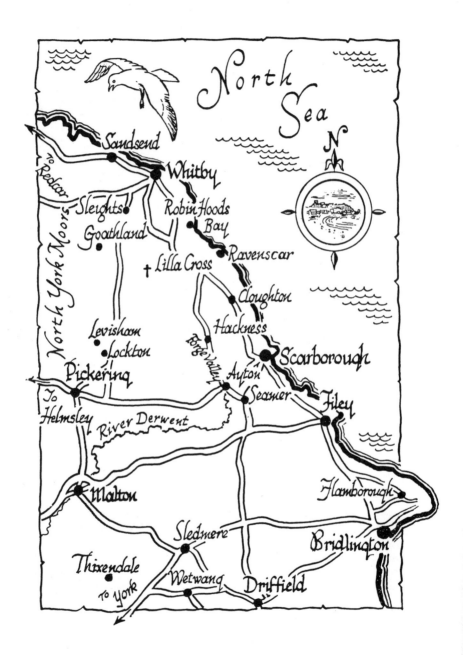

North Sea

N

To Redcar

Sandsend
Whitby

North York Moors

Sleights
Goathland

Robin Hoods Bay

† Lilla Cross

Ravenscar

Cloughton

Hackness

Levisham
Lockton

Forge Valley

Pickering

Ayton

Scarborough

To Helmsley

Seamer

Filey

River Derwent

Malton

Flamborough

Sledmere

Bridlington

Thixendale

To York

Wetwang

Driffield

Being close to Scarborough they have been popular with visitors for many years. The beauty of the River Derwent and the deep sided Forge Valley are attractions indeed. Close by can be found the ruins of Ayton castle, a fortified manor house of the Middle Ages.

In **Wykeham,** westward from Ayton, is the Georgian mansion of Wykeham Abbey on the site of a 12th century Cistercian nunnery. The historic village of **Brompton,** not far along the A170, was mentioned in the Domesday Book. William Wordsworth was married in the church in 1802, and here the 'father of aviation,' Sir George Cayley, had his family home.

Further inland is **Pickering.** Much of the area to the north of this part of the A170 is a Forest Park. The Forestry Commission has laid out many 'forest trails' and leaflets together with maps are widely available throughout the whole area. Pickering itself, which lies south of the forest areas, is truly the market town of the hinterland with its Norman castle, hostelries used by Cromwellian troops, Georgian and Victorian structures, a stage coach house visited by Charles Dickens, and a station now used by the North Yorkshire Moors Railway. The Railway Trust operates a service to Grosmont via the scenic Newton Dale and Goathland taking about one hour. The views from the train cannot be seen by road travellers, for the railway passes through a tremendous gorge carved 12,000 years ago by millions of gallons of water that had overflowed from a glacial lake in Eskdale.

South from Scarborough

Southward there are again two routes, the coastal A165 and the A171. The A166 leads to **Cayton Bay,** which once lay on the north side of an inland sea and is now an area of light industry and suburban dwellings. South of Cayton lies **Filey,** a small family resort which has kept most of its Victorian charm.

Between **Reighton** and **Speeton** are areas that cater for many caravanners and campers. Speeton has no access to the sea except down the vertical chalk cliffs. The church standing in a field has a funnel shaped belfry, the tower reputedly having been built by the Danes. The B1229 passes through **Bempton** where fine cliffs offer panoramic views to the north and south (extreme care is advised whilst on the cliff top). **Flamborough,** a large and expanding village, is fed by many roads, and from here visitors have a choice of bays and coves. The church dedicated to St. Oswald contains many interesting items.

To the south of Flamborough Head lies **Bridlington,** like Scarborough enjoying north and south beaches with broad sweeping promenades and having its own identity and appeal. The hinterland of Bridlington takes in the Wolds villages, and the network of roads and lanes is well signposted.

The B1253 passes through **Rudston.** Here in the churchyard stands a huge prehistoric monolith set up as a landmark. It is thought to have been deposited in ancient times by a melting glacier at a distance of ten miles away and moved by early man. To the north of Rudston the road runs through

North Burton (also known as Burton Fleming) to **Hummanby,** an attractive village. Although rapidly growing, it has neat cottages, fine restaurants and good inns. It lies south east of Filey, two miles from the sea. Hunmanby Hall dating from the 17th century was once the seat of the Osbaldstones and is now boarding school for girls.

To return to Scarborough, the road through Flixton and Staxton affords magnificent views and joins the A64 south of Seamer. The village of Seamer, lying four miles south of Scarborough, still holds annually an ancient fair, with reading of a charter and a ceremonial distribution of coins by the Lord of the Manor.

In this final section I have endeavoured to encourage the visitor to find joy in exploring the surrounding areas. There are many more villages apart from those listed. The chapter is intended to show the wide variety available, and the following books may be of interest to those who wish to know more:

Nikolaus Pevsner, *Buildings of England: Yorkshire, the North Riding.*
Barry Mitchell, *Exploring the Yorkshire Coast.*
Dalesman Books on Robin Hood's Bay, Whitby, Filey and Flamborough.
   Other sources of information are:
The Local Room, Scarborough Public Library.
The Tourist Information Centre, St. Nicholas Cliff, Scarborough.
The Forestry Commission, North East England, 14 Grosvenor Terrace, Bootham, York YO3 7BD.
National Park Information Office, Helmsley; or County Planning Officer, County Hall, Northallerton.

Whalebone archway, Whitby.